Building Lighthouses

Nellie Wilder

✳ Smithsonian

Consultants

Brian Mandell
Program Specialist
Smithsonian Science Education Center

Sara Cooper
Third Grade Teacher
Fullerton School District

Chrissy Johnson, M.Ed.
Teacher, Cedar Point Elementary
Prince William County Schools, Virginia

Publishing Credits

Rachelle Cracchiolo, M.S.Ed., *Publisher*
Conni Medina, M.A.Ed., *Editor in Chief*
Diana Kenney, M.A.Ed., NBCT, *Series Developer*
Emily R. Smith, M.A.Ed., *Content Director*
Véronique Bos, *Creative Director*
Robin Erickson, *Art Director*
Michelle Jovin, M.A., *Associate Editor*
Mindy Duits, *Series Designer*
Kevin Panter, *Senior Graphic Designer*
Smithsonian Science Education Center

Image Credits: p.13 Emad Victor Shenouda (Creative Commons); all other images from iStock and/or Shutterstock.

Library Congress Cataloging-in-Publication Data
Names: Rice, Dona, author. | Smithsonian Institution.
Title: Building lighthouses / Dona Herweck Rice ; Smithsonian.
Description: Huntington Beach, CA : Teacher Created Materials, [2020] | Copyrighted 2020 by the Smithsonian Institution. | Audience: K to grade 3.
  | Identifiers: LCCN 2018049787 (print) | LCCN 2018056069 (ebook) | ISBN 9781493868957 (eBook) | ISBN 9781493866557 (pbk.)
Subjects: LCSH: Lighthouses--Juvenile literature.
Classification: LCC VK1010 (ebook) | LCC VK1010 .R53 2020 (print) | DDC 387.1/55--dc23
LC record available at https://lccn.loc.gov/2018049787

Teacher Created Materials

5301 Oceanus Drive
Huntington Beach, CA 92649-1030
www.tcmpub.com
ISBN 978-1-4938-6655-7
© 2019 Teacher Created Materials, Inc.
Printed in Malaysia
Thumbprints.21249

Table of Contents

Let There Be Light

Ships at sea can travel far. But what if they get close to land? If it is **foggy** or dark, they may crash into a coast.

That is when lighthouses can help!

A lighthouse shines on a foggy morning.

People can see lighthouses during the day.

Lighthouses guide ships near coasts. The lights show **sailors** where to go. The lights also warn sailors of danger. Lighthouses are like traffic signs for sea travel.

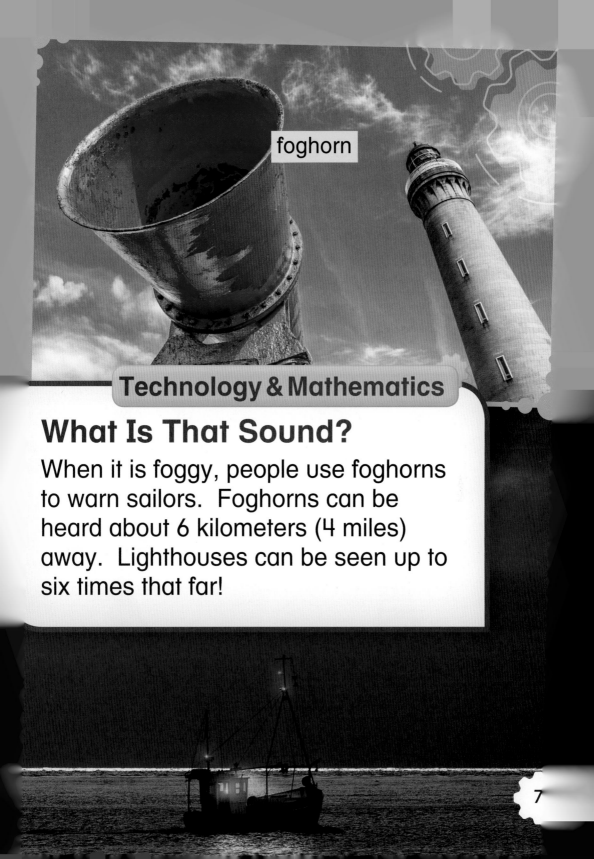

foghorn

Technology & Mathematics

What Is That Sound?

When it is foggy, people use foghorns to warn sailors. Foghorns can be heard about 6 kilometers (4 miles) away. Lighthouses can be seen up to six times that far!

Lighthouse History

Lighthouses are towers with bright lights at the tops. They shine out in the dark. In the day, they are markers so sailors can see where they are.

The Statue of Liberty was once used as a lighthouse.

erupting volcano

Nature Made

Nature can make lighthouses!
Volcanoes normally cannot be seen at
night. But they glow when they erupt.
Their glow can be used to guide ships.

Fire

Fire was the first light people used to guide ships. **Bonfires** helped sailors see land.

People later hung metal baskets from poles. They set fires in the baskets. This was the first type of lighthouse.

bonfire

This was the first type of lighthouse.

Pharos

People think the first lighthouse was called Pharos. It had mirrors at the top. During the day, sunlight bounced off the mirrors. At night, people lit fires at the top. Its light could be seen from far away.

How do you say that?
Pharos = (FAIR-ohs)

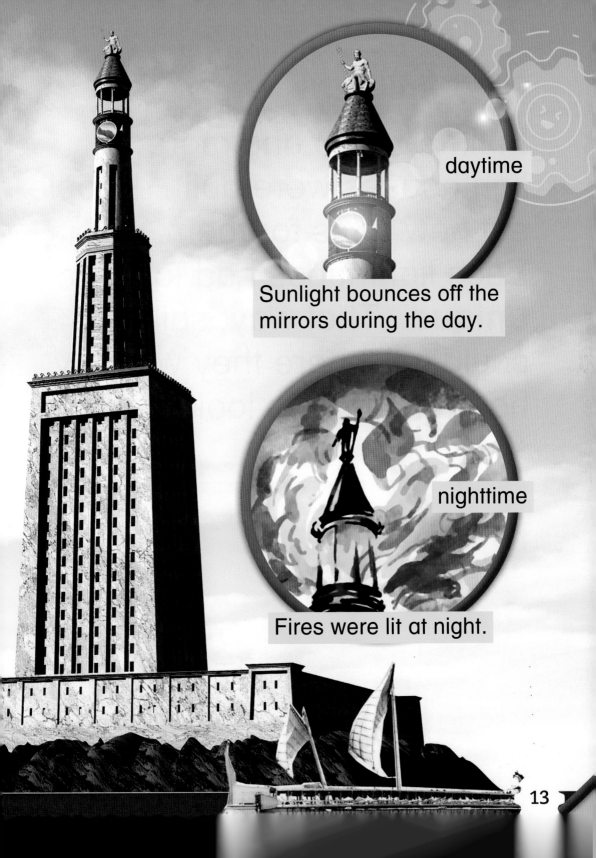

daytime

Sunlight bounces off the mirrors during the day.

nighttime

Fires were lit at night.

New Rules

In time, more and more lighthouses were built. People set new rules for them. Each lighthouse had to be **unique**. That way, sailors could tell where they were by how lighthouses looked.

The paint on this lighthouse helps it stand out.

Design

Each lighthouse was built with things found in the area. It was then painted to stand out. The colors depended on where it was built.

New Ways

Lighthouses are not built like they used to be. There is new **technology**. Computers are used to build them now. No one needs to run lighthouses like they used to. The old ways are in the past.

This lighthouse was built many years ago.

This lighthouse uses power from the sun to shine its light.

Stories to Tell

Lighthouses can be found on almost any coast. They are all unique. They have saved ships and sailors. If they could speak, what stories do you think they would tell?

STEAM CHALLENGE

The Problem

A new lighthouse is needed on the coast. You have been asked to design it. It should be unique. It must shine its light for a long distance. Are you up to the task?

The Goals

- Use any materials to build a model of your lighthouse.
- Use a flashlight to act as the light.
- Use your lighthouse in a dark room to test it.

Research and Brainstorm

What do modern lighthouses use for light? How can light be seen from far away?

Design and Build

Draw your plan. How will it work? What materials will you use? Build your model!

Test and Improve

Place a flashlight inside your lighthouse. Turn on the flashlight. Turn off all other lights. Can you see the light from the other side of the room? Can you make the lighthouse better? Try again.

Reflect and Share

What else besides light and sound could help ships near the shore? How can people driving cars stay safe when it is dark or foggy?

Glossary

bonfires

foggy

sailors

technology

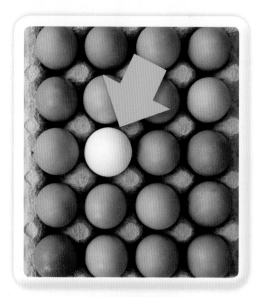

unique

Career Advice
from Smithsonian

Do you want to design lighthouses? Here are some tips to get you started.

"Study arts to learn how to design and build lighthouses."
— Sharon Park, Assistant Director of the Smithsonian's Architectural & Historic Preservation

"I love lighthouses because I love history. All old buildings were new at one time. If you study them closely enough, you can see how people lived and worked." *— Michael Lawrence, Assistant Director for Exhibitions*